A Pictorial History
Leavenworth

Foreword

By Pat Morris

The fortunes of many who came west were reflected in the lives of those who settled in Icicle Valley.

First, a scattering of farms after clearing away the trees. Then a town with a fairly fluid population where, because of their jobs, railroaders were moved frequently. Businesses that were chiefly saloons supported by railroad wages. Single men and young families with few beyond middle age made up its residents.

Next, a ballooning of the town as a major industry from Iowa brought hundreds to work in the logging woods and sawmill. Soon afterward, the realization that fruit could be raised here brought additional change. The division of large tracts of land into five or ten acre plots commenced. Increased settlement as orchards went in on these subdivision and enlarged the valley's population.

The town was hard hit by the calling up of nearly one hundred young men for the military during World War I. Raising fruit did not prove as profitable as hoped. The switchyard facility was moved to Wenatchee in 1922. The sawmill closure in 1927 meant the loss of hundreds of jobs. Loss of the town's railroad connection was a heavy blow.

The Great Depression set in. The Trinity mine closed, leaving more out of work. A good many young men were called away for military service in the '40s. War work caused an exodus, as the defense industries offered better pay.

By the 1960s with a population seriously divided by a school site issue, it was time for a change. The LIFE study and the work of many individuals who saw an opportunity to bolster the failing economy, through a "pull yourself up by your own bootstraps" program, accomplished even more than originally hoped for and created the town as you see it today.

Table of Contents

Views

Those who first saw western Chelan County found it heavily wooded with little flat land available for farming. The coming of the railroad opened Tumwater Canyon and beyond to exploration and settlement; the town started in 1892 as the railroad built through along the right-of-way. It was small in size, had dirt streets and its store fronts were the usual high false fronts common about 1900. It had neither water, sewer nor electricity.

As the town grew, fires cleared away much that had formerly been there. Brick buildings replaced the wooden ones. The sawmill company dammed the river and furnished water and lights to the town. Eventually a park took the place of the unsightliness along the right-of-way.

Expansion of the switchyard to accommodate construction of the dam in Tumwater Canyon greatly enhanced the rail facility. Wages from the sawmill and the railroad gave the town its first real burst of prosperity.

As automobiles came into common use about 1920 a demand for better roads and paved streets began. The removal of the railroad out of Tumwater Canyon and a state and federal move to fund major highway construction, although a good many years passed in accomplishing these goals, connected Eastern Washington with the western portion.

During this same period orchard plantings figured largely. Productive land was made even more desirable by irrigation. Farmers' cooperatives were formed to market the apples, pears and summer fruits the new plantings bore. Log cabin homes gave way before fine residences and automobiles replaced horses and buggies. Homesteading and pioneering were largely left behind as individuals with money from the East purchased portions of the older farms and set in fruit trees.

LEFT: View of Leavenworth looking east, circa 1915. *Courtesy Chris Rader Collection*

Main St.,
Leavenworth, Wash.

LEFT: View of downtown
Leavenworth, 1910. Old
Settlers Group volunteered
to clean up the park. *Courtesy
Chamber of Commerce Collection*

ABOVE: Main Street in
Leavenworth, circa 1890.
Courtesy John and Betty Rogers Collection

RIGHT: Main Street in
Leavenworth, early 1900s.
Courtesy John and Betty Rogers Collection

ABOVE: Main Street in Leavenworth, circa 1908. *Courtesy John and Betty Rogers Collection*

BELOW: Main Street in Leavenworth, 1909. The buildings on the park side of the street were on Great Northern Railroad right of way. When railroad officials insisted the area be cleaned up, the buildings were removed. *Courtesy Chris Rader Collection*

LEFT: View of the Wenatchee River through Tumwater Canyon near Leavenworth. *Courtesy Bill Haines Collection*

FAR ABOVE: The North Road, circa 1933. *Courtesy Karl Pflugrath Collection*

NEAR ABOVE: View of Leavenworth, 1918. The Motteler Building is in the foreground. *Courtesy Chamber of Commerce Collection*

NEAR BELOW: Phelps Creek mine near Lyman Glacier, circa 1935. *Courtesy Blackburn Family Collection*
FAR BELOW: View of the Wenatchee River through Tumwater Canyon near Leavenworth. *Courtesy Bill Haines Collection*
RIGHT: The original Leavenworth City Hall was on Commercial St. where Cascade Medical Center is today. The corner of Ninth St. is on the right where the Tumwater Inn Restaurant and Lounge is located today.

LEFT: An outing to Horseshoe Lake, July 4, 1926, by Reg and Jessie Parsons, Mr. and Mrs. George Gardner, Jack Miller and Pete Taylor. Members of the group are seen center of photograph on bank of lake. *Upper Valley Museum at Leavenworth / WVM&CC / Parsons Collection #003-77-9*

ABOVE: Front Street, Leavenworth, 1930s. *Upper Valley Museum at Leavenworth / WVM&CC / Parsons Collection #003-77-11*

ABOVE: The Lamb-Davis mill with the Peavine log train aproaching. *Courtesy Byron Dickinson Collection*

BELOW: Early Leavenworth looking south in the early 1900s. *Courtesy Byron Dickinson Collection*
RIGHT: A 1920s picture of Cresent Beach on Lake Wenatchee. *Courtesy Byron Dickinson Collection*

LEFT: Downtown Leavenworth, circa 1910. *Courtesy Byron Dickinson Collection*
BELOW LEFT: Lyman Lake, circa 1930. *Courtesy Blackburn Family Collection*
NEAR BELOW: A historic overview of early Leavenworth with the dam, log pond and Lamb-Davis sawmill in 1913. *Courtesy Byron Dickinson Collection*
FAR BELOW: Chiwawa Mountain and Lyman Lake. *Courtesy Blackburn Family Collection*

LEFT: Snow in Leavenworth, circa 1936. *Courtesy Chamber of Commerce Collection*

ABOVE: Civilian Conservation Corps, Camp Icicle, 983rd Company, Stevens Pass, Side Camp, circa 1935. *Courtesy Upper Valley Museum at Leavenworth/WVM&CC/C.C.C. Collection #003-82-135*

OPPOSITE: The Alps in Tumwater Canyon, circa 1931. *Courtesy Archie Marlin Collection*
FAR ABOVE: R.B. Field's Arabian horses graze in the pasture below the Field home.
NEAR ABOVE: Icicle Ridge Lookout. *Courtesy Byron Dickinson Collection*
RIGHT: View of the Wenatchee River in Tumwater Canyon near Leavenworth. *Courtesy Bill Haines Collection*

LEFT: Sunitsch Cabin built in the 1880s. *Courtesy Ann Gabrielson Collection*
BELOW: The original home in Sunitsch Canyon built at the turn of the century by Mathias Sunitsch. The barn was built a few years later by Charles Bement. The barn and the milkhouse are still standing. *Courtesy Ann Gabrielson Collection*

Left: Mr. and Mrs. Gutherless at their home. *Courtesy Bill Haines Collection*

Below Left: Red Mountain Ole's original cabin at Phelps Creek. Photo taken in 1930. The cabin burned down and he rebuilt on the same creek. *Courtesy Blackburn Family Collection*

Below Right: Red Mountain Ole's second cabin at Phelps Creek, circa 1934. *Courtesy Blackburn Family Collection*

OPPOSITE: The W.W. Hatmaker family and their dog "Tippy" at 518 Birch St. Their home was built in 1904 by Mr. Weigand, who built the former Hub, later Ruth's Dress Shop, later Tannenbaum. Leona and William's children were Charlie, Roy, Oscar, David, Hazel and Peggy. Some of the children are pictured.

FAR ABOVE: Interior of the Lamb-Davis home, early 1900s. *Courtesy Upper Valley Museum at Leavenworth Collection*

NEAR ABOVE: Lamb-Davis bungalow. *Courtesy Upper Valley Museum at Leavenworth Collection*

ABOVE RIGHT: Jess Pendleton in Pendleton Canyon which was named after him and his homestead. Photo, circa 1919. *Courtesy Bill Haines Collection*

RIGHT: The Gutherless residence in the winter, circa 1905. *Courtesy Bill Haines Collection*

Commerce & Industry

The first major industry in Icicle Valley was the railroad. As it grew and traffic burgeoned once the Depression of 1893 passed, businesses that met the needs of railroaders and their families went in. Wages were good and the employment steady. The coming of the sawmill complex in 1903 turned attention to the great stands of fir and pine nearby. The river furnished transport for the log cut along the Wenatchee and its tributary streams; a logging railroad also brought the product of the woods to Icicle Valley. At one time the firm employed over one thousand men in its operations. The huge demand for fruit boxes in the county furnished a market locally and car after car of lumber was sent east, as well.

These two major sources of income brought businessmen to furnish food, housing and entertainment for the workers. For a good many decades the horse as the main source of transportation

was an established way of life with blacksmith and livery barns catering to them.

We must not forget the produce of the outlying farming region where stock raising, hay and dairy products boosted the economy. As orchards came into bearing, the preparing and storage of fruit for market eventually meant cooperatives and warehouses. Automobiles and all that catered to the supply of the needs for such vehicles came to become a business in the town.

Always the belief that a major mineral find lay undiscovered in the unknown mountains of the Cascades attracted prospectors or pack strings to supply development work were usual and furnished businesses with another outlet before 1920. Once a bridge on the river and a trail to Blewett mining camp were built, a stage connection and a means of shipping gold by railroad and becoming the supplier of miners' needs aided early businesses. For several decades the work of the Royal Development Company on the Chiwawa River employed numbers, as the deposits of that region were developed.

LEFT: Bill Walton's poolhall on Front Street, June 20, 1922. Rein Templin on the left, Wilson Walton center, Bill Walton on the right. *Courtesy Howard Templin Collection*

ABOVE: The Lamb-Davis Lumber Company built a dam across the Wenatchee River creating a mill pond upstream. Downtown Leavenworth is in the background. Photo taken in 1904. *Courtesy Byron Dickinson Collection*

BELOW: The Lamb-Davis mill was built in 1904 and became one of the largest inland sawmills in the world at that time. Mountain Home is in the background. *Courtesy Byron Dickinson Collection*

ABOVE RIGHT: Looking west from the mill pond up the jack rig of the Lamb-Davis sawmill. *Courtesy Byron Dickinson Collection*

BELOW RIGHT: "Falling Crew", Civilian Conservation Corps, Camp Icicle, 983rd Company, circa 1935. Standing: Phil Scoog, Albert Brown, Hank Robertson, Frank Lapine, Rae Reed, Art Morris (boss), Punk, Art Cass, Perry Elliot. Front row: unknown, unknown, unknown, Swede Johnson, Ja Fansler, Chuck Burgess, unknown. *Courtesy Upper Valley Museum at Leavenworth / WVM&CC / C.C.C Collection #003-82-136*

BELOW: Two sawyers use a crosscut saw on a tree to be felled. *Courtesy Dennis Pobst Collection*
RIGHT: A cedar bolt drive on the White River. Settlers cut the cedar trees, split them into bolts and float them to Lake Wenatchee for milling. *Courtesy Byron Dickinson Collection*

ABOVE LEFT: This sawmill, built in 1911 by W.W. Burgess, provided lumber for many Upper Valley homes and barns. *Courtesy Byron Dickinson Collection*

LEFT: Logs were skidded to the river in the winter months, held and then released in the spring floods. They travelled down the Wenatchee River to the log pond at the Lamb-Davis saw mill. *Courtesy Byron Dickinson Collection*

ABOVE RIGHT: Loading with a still boom jammer onto an early log truck. *Courtesy Dennis Pobst Collection*

ABOVE LEFT: River drivers used pike poles, peaveys and occasionally dynamite to break up log jams on the Wenatchee River. *Courtesy Byron Newell Collection*

BELOW LEFT: Jack Burgess and Sid Fritz test a new invention, the chain saw. *Courtesy Byron Newell Collection*

FAR ABOVE: Horse logging in the 1920s. George Shugart is on top of the load, and W.O. Burgess is in back of the horses. *Courtesy Byron Newell Collection*

NEAR ABOVE: The Merritt Lodge. *Courtesy Byron Newell Collection*

FAR ABOVE: The Crescent Beach Store at Lake Wenatchee on June 21, 1938. *Courtesy Byron Dickinson Collection*

NEAR ABOVE: The first gas and grocery store in Plain. *Courtesy Byron Dickinson Collection*

RIGHT: The stiff boom jammer was was one of the early steps towards mechanized logging machinery. Prior to this all logging was done by hand or with horses. *Courtesy Byron Dickinson Collection*

ABOVE: Prusky Logging, Henry and Elva Prusky and George Kirkpatrick. Family photo.
LEFT: A log truck being loaded with a hayrack up the White River in 1962. *Courtesy Byron Dickinson Collection*
BELOW: The Pobst family baling hay in the 1940s. *Courtesy Byron Dickinson Collection*

ABOVE LEFT: Rein F. Templin on left and W.E. Williams at the Templin's blacksmith shop on Commercial Street, 1907. *Courtesy Howard Templin Collection*

FAR ABOVE: Dude Brown, Rein Templin, Fred Brender, circa 1905. *Courtesy Stan Harrison Collection*

NEAR ABOVE: Tholin home on Commercial Street. It is now the Gingerbread Factory.

LEFT: Brender's Blacksmith shop, early 1900s. *Courtesy Chamber of Commerce Collection*

LEFT: Anderson Meat Market, circa 1905. Left to right: Rein Templin, Bill Anderson, Mr. Daley, and Mr. Schott. *Courtesy Howard Templin Collection*

NEAR BELOW: The Overland Hotel which provided every convinience such as hot and cold water on every floor, lavatories, both rooms and others that are usually found in a first class hotel. Photo circa 1915. *Courtesy Leavenworth Echo Collection*

FAR BELOW: The Hotel Clifford, 1905. *Courtesy Leavenworth Echo Collection*

LEFT: U.S. Army office building at Civilian Conservation Corps, Camp Icicle, 983rd Company, circa 1937. Today the location of the camp is known as Sleeping Lady Conference Retreat. *Courtesy Upper Valley Museum at Leavenworth / WVM&CC / Hanna Collection #004-27-1.17*

BELOW LEFT: Racket Store and City Drug Store, 1905. This was the first building erected after the fire of June 8, 1904. *Courtesy Leavenworth Echo Collection*

BELOW: This building was a bar, opera house, City Hall and gift shop at different times. Today the building houses the Village Pharmacy. Photo 1905. *Courtesy Leavenworth Echo Collection*

RIGHT: Leavenworth Market. *Courtesy Gretchen Minard Collection*

BELOW RIGHT: The original Leavenworth Echo, 1905. *Courtesy Leavenworth Echo Collection*

OPPOSITE: Rein F. Templin's blacksmith shop on Commercial Street, 1907. Rein Templin is on the left. *Courtesy Howard Templin Collection*

ABOVE LEFT: Inside an early Leavenworth business. *Courtesy John and Betty Rogers Collection*

LEFT: Leavenworth State Bank which opened July 8, 1910. *Courtesy Upper Valley Museum at Leavenworth Collection*

ABOVE RIGHT: Lamb-Davis mill pond, 1908. *Courtesy Bill Haines Collection*

RIGHT: Blewett Mining Camp, circa 1902. *Courtesy Bill Haines Collection*

ABOVE: Construction begins on the Lamb-Davis dam. Homes on Main St., Ninth St. and Commercial St. are visible in the background.

"SQUARE DEAL" GROCERY
(QUALITY FOODS FOR LESS)

PHONE 25   FREE DELIVERY

Leavenworth, Wash., 3-2   193 4

M Mrs. Sunitsch

No.

Reg. No.	Clerk	ACCOUNT FORWARDED	
1	lettuce		15
2	lemons		35
3	Gelatine		25
4	pineapple		22
5	celery		10
6			
7			1 07
8			
9			
10			
11			
12			
13			
14	3		

LEFT: Dudley Wilson with logging team "Red" and "Snip," 1946. *Courtesy Judy Wyssen Collection*
ABOVE: Early grocery receipt, 1934. *Courtesy Ann Gabrielson Collection*

ABOVE: Anderson's Lodging was the first structure built in Leavenworth. At 917 Commercial St., today it is Mrs. Anderson's Lodging House.

ABOVE & RIGHT: William F. Rhode and helper on the Great Northern telegraph line on Stevens Pass.

ABOVE RIGHT: The Great Northern Lumber Company, circa 1930, formerly the Lamb-Davis Lumber Company until 1915. *Courtesy Chamber of Commerce Collection*

Report of the Financial Condition of

The Leavenworth State Bank

Leavenworth, Washington

December 31, 1952

RESOURCES		LIABILITIES	
Loans and discounts	$675,972.69	Capital Stock	100,000.00
Overdrafts	191.31		
Banking House	28,202.79	Surplus	50,000.00
Furniture and fixtures	2,476.06		
Other bonds	3,000.00	Undivided profits	37,437.63
Life Ins. Policies (Actual cash value exceeds $10,000.00)	1.00		
U. S. Bonds	1,405,155.00	Reserves	11,522.88
Municipal bonds & warrants	235,390.57		
Cash and due from banks 628,328.07	2,268,873.64	Deposits	2,779,756.98
	2,978,717.49		2,978,717.49

Officers

R. B. Field, President
Thos. J. Day, Vice President
Henry Woldtvet, Cashier
Hazel Hansen, Asst. Cashier

Directors

R. B. Field   Thos. J. Day

Henry Woldtvet

R. J. Smith   John W. McCoy

Deposits in this bank are insured by the Federal Deposit Insurance Corporation up to $10,000.00 in the manner and to the extent provided under the terms of the Banking Act.

ABOVE: LSB financial statement, 1932.
RIGHT: R.B. Field, second from left, who established the Leavenworth State Bank on July 8, 1920, was honored when the bank became the Seattle-First Nation Bank. At left is Wayne Lanphere, and on R.B.'s left are Clarence Hummel and Frank Jerome.

RIGHT: Ken and Otis Buzard with marten they trapped at French Creek up the Icicle, 1945. *Courtesy Leah Wilson-Smith Collection*

NEAR BELOW: John B. "JB" Adams standing in front of his office building in Leavenworth, circa 1910. John and Mary Adams arrived in Leavenworth with daughter Mildred and son John "Jay" in 1894 when the railroad built a grade to Chiwaukum. Youngest son William "Willie" C. born December of 1894 died November of 1896 from a fall from the family home's front porch. Jay became Chelan County Superior Court Judge. Note signage on widows: "ADAMS & CARR REAL". *Wenatchee Valley Museum & Cultural Center / Adams Collection #84-30-6*

FAR BELOW: The Cougar Inn, 1927. *Courtesy Bill Haines Collection*

People

In 1900 Leavenworth was a village with less than five hundred population. Lawlessness was a problem. With the coming of a sizeable number from Iowa, as the sawmill there transferred operations to Icicle Valley, the big step toward town incorporation was taken. It was largely aimed at bringing under control the distaff element accustomed to carousing about the saloons. Such individuals as Deed Mayar, newspaper editor, Dr. George Hoxsey, railroad physician, John B. Adams and numbers of others who served on the City Council or even as mayor helped shape the town as did colorful lawman "Dude" Brown.

The first settlers, who came to take up land and farm, and the numbers of railroaders who lived here briefly each left their special stamp. To the influx of Iowa folk, Tennessee woods workers, Midwesterners, who came to grow the famous Big, Red Apple, a good many local folks trace their family lines.

Schools were important and beginning with a one-month session taught by Ed Balch, have grown, improved, kept pace with expansion. After two school terms that were held in abandoned stores from the railroad work, the first big frame, a two story beauty on present Forestry grounds was built. Oddly enough, it was used little more than a dozen years before the influx of sawmill families made a larger facility necessary. The new school was our first brick building; a high school joined it within a few years. Both of these buildings faced Evans Street. A large gymnasium was added by 1920. Later a grade school went up at this site and the first and second bricks were torn down.

With consolidation from outlying districts new structures went in beyond the residential district and at Peshastin. The one-room school, a reminder of early days at Winton, was moved to a new larger one at Plain.

A colorful part of our valley's history centers around the federal program instituted in the 1930s to train youth and provided jobs known as the Civilian Conservation Corps. Their camp was erected along the Icicle River south of town. For nearly a decade the sight of Army trucks hauling supplies in or transporting the young men to assignments in the woods or to fight forest fires was a familiar part of valley life.

LEFT: Jim Evans' girls, circa 1940. Left to right: Muriel, Ruth, Sally and Marion. *Courtesy Carol Thorson Collection*

ABOVE: Frances and R.B. Field. *Courtesy Upper Valley Museum Collection*

LEFT: Spare time at the Civilian Conservation Corps 983rd Company at Camp Icicle, F-29, circa 1935. Today the location of the camp is known as Sleeping Lady Mt. Retreat Center. *Courtesy Upper Valley Museum at Leavenworth / WVM&CC / C.C.C Collection #003-82-84*

BELOW: Early pioneers in the Plain Valley. *Courtesy Byron Dickinson Collection*

BELOW LEFT: Stevens family.

LEFT & BELOW: The Gutherless family. They lived near the railroad in Tumwater Canyon. Mrs. Gutherless created this "baby carriage" to push her children four miles to town on the tracks when the train wasn't running. Photo, circa 1915. *Courtesy Bill Haines Collection*

LEFT: Alta (lower right), Floyd Williams (second from right) and friends, circa 1910. *Courtesy Fran Wise Collection*

FAR ABOVE: Floyd Williams and Dick Simons, circa 1910. *Courtesy Fran Wise Collection*

NEAR ABOVE: Harry Wall, right, was later the owner of Chelan Box and Manufacturing Company. *Courtesy Fran Wise Collection*

FAR ABOVE: The Lake Wenatchee Schoolhouse in 1920. Later it became the Lake Wenatchee Grange Hall. *Courtesy Byron Dickinson Collection*

NEAR ABOVE: Built at a cost of 16,000 dollars, this first brick school building in town stood where the Cascade School District parking lot is now. *Courtesy Byron Dickinson Collection*

ABOVE RIGHT: Alta Williams and her baby, circa 1915. *Courtesy Fran Wise Collection*

BELOW RIGHT: In 1912 a larger schoolhouse was built in Plain and was used until 1951. It also served as a church and community center for the area. *Courtesy Byron Dickinson Collection*

LEFT: During the big snow of 1917 youngsters could earn good money by trekking between Leavenworth and Plain carrying products of necessity. Ralph O' Dell is pictured. *Courtesy Byron Dickinson Collection*

BELOW LEFT: Winifred Stephen, 1923. *Courtesy Karl Pflugrath Collection*

BELOW: Otto Kenyan, an early businessman in Leavenworth. *Courtesy Byron Dickinson Collection*

ABOVE LEFT: Mathias Sunitsch, 1923. He homesteaded Sunitsh Canyon in the early 1880s. He came from Austria. *Courtesy Ann Gabrielson Collection*
ABOVE RIGHT: Mable (Bement) Sunitsch and George Sunitsch, Kathryn Sunitsch, and Franz Sunitsch, 1923. *Courtesy Ann Gabrielson Collection*
RIGHT: Rein Templin, 1925. *Courtesy Stan Harrison Collection*

FAR LEFT: Leavenworth students, 1915.

NEAR LEFT: Red Mountain Ole with pelts on the trail. *Courtesy Blackburn Family Collection*

BELOW LEFT: Franz Sunitsch with his purebred holstein "Lady Fair." He is preparing for the Leavenworth Chelan County Fair. Photo, 1928. *Courtesy Ann Gabrielson Collection*

BELOW: Lora Buzard took this picture of her children Doug and Charlotte, 1931. *Courtesy Leah Wilson-Smith Collection*

ABOVE: A funeral service for Red Mountain Ole' who died July 10, 1934. *Courtesy Blackburn Family Collection*

FAR LEFT: Magnus Bakke cutting firewood for the cookstove at home. The house was at 413 Ski Hill Drive. Photo, 1935. *Courtesy Kjell Bakke Collection*

MIDDLE LEFT: Trinna King Burgess, early school teacher in Plain. *Courtesy Byron Dickinson Collection*

NEAR LEFT: Magnus Bakke as fire guard at Merritt Guard Station, 1936. He is with his wife Inga and daughters, Marie and Ethel, and sons, Kjell standing in front of his dad and Knute in arms of his mother. Mr. And Mrs. Kjosnes at left. *Courtesy Kjell Bakke Collection*

RIGHT: Leavenworth High School class of 1937. *Courtesy Chamber of Commerce Collection*

LEFT: Ben Costello on Prospect and Cherry Street, 1941. Ben and Charlotte grew up in Leavenworth and graduated from Leavenworth High School. *Courtesy Leah Wilson-Smith Collection*

BELOW: Dudley Wilson is home for Christmas from winter trapping, December 24, 1946. *Courtesy Judy Wyssen Collection*

ABOVE RIGHT: Dodging fans and flying confetti, Jim and Carol Adamson begin a married life together in 1947. The wedding was held at the Methodist Church in Leavenworth. The building, on the southwest corner of Evans and Whitman streets, is a residence today, *Courtesy Byron Dickinson Collection*

BELOW RIGHT: Viola Wilson and daughters Mildred, Judy and Leah in front of their home on Prospect Street, 1947. *Courtesy Judy Wyssen Collection*

Public Service

Leavenworth has been fortunate to have doctors and medical care since early times. Injuries among railroad workers or in the woods work were at first treated in hotel rooms. Then private hospitals were erected by individual doctors; five were widely used, as epidemics and injuries required them. Surgery was little known among the early physicians here and even appendicitis cases were sent by train to large cities. Babies were delivered at home.

About 1920 Dr. Albert Lessing and banker Robert Field commenced a drive for a major hospital facility. Cascade Sanitarium was built with benefiting patients with lung diseases in mind. The construction of the eight-mile tunnel and new rail line with attendant accidents forced its enlargement as the numbers of patients burgeoned. Women began to demand medical care in a hospital for the birthing of children. Trained doctors who performed surgeries were added. Eventually a much larger hospital near the first was constructed and is in use at the present time.

From the incorporation of the town in 1906 mayors and city officials were elected. A city hall, fire hall and jail building was erected in 1906, the original one standing until 1938. A larger building was purchased on Front Street in the 1930s with library and Boy Scout facilities in mind. After much altercation, the big brick saloon was converted into city hall number two and used until quite recent times. Today's modern Bavarian-styled building along Highway 2 houses the town library, City Council rooms, sheriff and city offices.

LEFT: The Cascade Sanitarium, circa 1923. The steps of the sanitarium continued on the other side of Main Street down to the Wenatchee River. *Courtesy Rena Stroup Collection*

ABOVE: Benchmark Mountain Lookout. These lookouts were manned for locating forest fires. *Courtesy Byron Dickinson Collection*

ABOVE RIGHT: Town Marshal Dude Brown, circa 1919. *Courtesy Chris Rader Collection*

BELOW RIGHT: Plain's first post office was small enough to be moved to the home of whoever was postmaster at the time. *Courtesy Byron Dickinson Collection*

LEFT: Early firefighters pose for a picture. *Courtesy Byron Dickinson Collection*

FAR ABOVE: A 1920s forest ranger at the Rock Creek Guard Station. *Courtesy Byron Dickinson Collection*

NEAR ABOVE: Falling Crew; Civilian Conservation Corps Camp Icicle, Leavenworth, Washington; circa 1935. Standing: Phil Scoog, Albert Brown, Hank Robertson, Frank Lapine, Rae Reed, Art Morris (boss), Punk, Art Cass, Perry Elliot; Front row: unknown, unknown, unknown, Swede Johnson, Ja Fansler, Chuck Burgess, unknown. *Upper Valley Museum at Leavenworth / WVM&CC / C.C.C Collection #003-82-136*

NEAR RIGHT: Joe Guiberson, Superintendent; Civilian Conservation Corps cabins in background; Camp Icicle, Leavenworth, Washington; circa 1935. *Upper Valley Museum at Leavenworth / WVM&CC / C.C.C Collection #003-82-68*

FAR RIGHT: Left to right: Mr. Keller, Ed. Adv.; Mr. Joe Guiberson, Superintendent; Doc Martin, doctor; General Stone; Major Hirsch; Lt. Brown, 2nd in command; Civilian Conservation Corps Camp Icicle, Leavenworth, Washington; circa 1935. *Upper Valley Museum at Leavenworth / WVM&CC / C.C.C Collection #003-82-69*

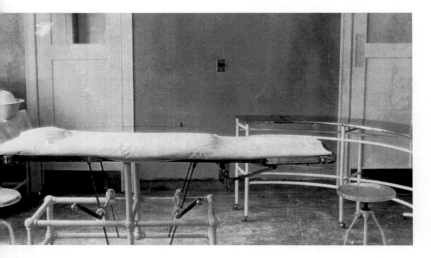

ABOVE: The first operating room in Leavenworth at the Cascade Sanitarium, circa 1923. *Courtesy Rena Stroup Collection*

LEFT: Kjell Bakke, 2nd Lt., 1957. He served 32 years in the U.S. Army Reserve and retired as a full Colonel. *Courtesy Kjell Bakke Collection*

RIGHT: Howard L. "Hoppy" Hopkins, an early physician at the Cascade Sanitarium. He died in 1957 of cancer as a result of X-ray burns on his little finger. The cancer spread rapidly to his brain. *Courtesy Rena Stroup Collection*

RIGHT: A group of Forest Service officials meeting at the old Dirty Face Lodge on Lake Wenatchee. The first forest supervisor was Hal Sylvester, who is fourth from the right. *Courtesy Byron Dickinson Collection*

BELOW LEFT: Water commissioner Henry Harrison at Leavenworth's new city pump, circa 1950. *Courtesy Stan Harrison Collection*

BELOW RIGHT: Muriel Evans (Thorson) in nurses training for WWII. *Courtesy Carol Thorson Collection*

Transportation

Early roads in our area were largely built by settlers. Even as late as 1924 most were one-lane dirt traces useful mostly during dry summer weather for horse traffic. Not until the 1920s was an effort made to connect the county by a practical route with the first Cascade Mountain pass, Snoqualmie. A vigorous program of federal and state aid in the 1930 opened a way across by Stevens Pass. Tumwater Canyon's abandoned railroad right-of-way was added to the state road system and in great measure mitigated the town's loss of the railroad.

As the cross-state road system went in, tourism in the form of ski jumping tourneys and development of a tourist park attracted those who came by auto.

For a good many years at the town's start, horses were the local means of transport. Trips to Wenatchee or more distant spots were by train. Even with the first cars, little traveling was done in winter or during the muddy seasons. It was time to celebrate when streets and outlying roads were leveled, graveled and oil applied to lay the dust. When the town afforded paving, residents really felt "citified". Winter snowplowing was an additional refinement.

Adopting a portion of the former railroad right-of-way for part of a highway moved the city to connect the portions of town on either side. The bridge across the Wenatchee River outside of town built in the 1930s completed the connection with the two mountain passes. Good roads brought tourists through to the town to enjoy our scenery, sports and sunshine.

LEFT: Floyd Williams on the track to Tumwater Canyon out of Leavenworth.
Courtesy Fran Wise Collection

ABOVE: A view of a train passing through Leavenworth, 1900. *Courtesy Bill Haines Collection*

ABOVE: R.B. Field, right, and a friend in a horse-drawn sleigh on Front Street, 1902. *Courtesy Upper Valley Museum at Leavenworth Collection*

LEFT: Early horse drawn carriage, circa 1903. *Courtesy Fran Wise Collection*

ABOVE: Railroad employees, circa 1910. Floyd J. Williams is in the middle. *Courtesy Fran Wise Collection*

RIGHT: Photo of an engine, circa 1910. Daniel J. Nicholson, with the large hat on, is standing on the very front of the engine. *Courtesy Chris Orcutt Collection*

ABOVE LEFT: A group of Wenatchee socialites riding the Peavine Railroad on an outing. From all accounts it was a wonderful success. *Courtesy Byron Dickinson Collection*

LEFT: Great Northern Railroad yard, early 1900s. *Courtesy Milton Wagy Collection*

ABOVE: R.B. Field at the wheel of an early automobile. *Courtesy Upper Valley Museum at Leavenworth Collection*

OPPOSITE: A group of people on a train. Floyd and Alta Williams on the left. *Courtesy Fran Wise Collection*

ABOVE: The results of 150 kegs of gun powder in a snow slide, circa 1915. *Courtesy Chamber of Commerce Collection*

ABOVE LEFT: Leo J. Bodvin with the new Highcar. *Courtesy Leo H. Bodvin Collection*
LEFT: The new Highcar and crewmembers somewhere east of the Cascade Tunnel. *Courtesy Leo H. Bodvin Collection*
ABOVE: The new Highcar on the road, Harry Root in front. *Courtesy Leo H. Bodvin Collection*

ABOVE LEFT: Echo Point, Blewett Pass. *Courtesy Leo H. Bodvin Collection*

LEFT: The early 1940s Highcar and crew. Leo J. Bodvin, is on the far right. Second from left is Harry Root, the foreman of the crew. *Courtesy Leo H. Bodvin Collection*

ABOVE: Tumwater entrance. The graveled road over Stevens Pass that opened in 1929 was cause for great publicity. Photo circa 1930.

NEAR BELOW: Hoffman Gas Station. *Courtesy Leo H. Bodvin Collection*
FAR BELOW: Clearing snow on Stevens Pass. *Courtesy Leo H. Bodvin Collection*
RIGHT: Roy Hatmaker ran the Shell Service Station on US 2 (Gustav's Restaurant) 1940. *Courtesy Leo H. Bodvin Collection*

ABOVE: Josephine Lindston and the Lindston children, Agnes, Ovidia and James at the summit of Blewett Pass, September 11, 1918. *Courtesy Blackburn Family Collection*

BELOW: Blewett Pass ten miles east of the summit, circa 1925. *Courtesy Bill Haines Collection*

OPPOSITE: The official opening of Stevens Pass in Tumwater Canyon, observed by a caravan of 283 cars, July 11, 1925. *Courtesy Joyce and Earl Johnson Collection*

NEAR BELOW: Slide on Stevens Pass; February 1935. *Upper Valley Museum at Leavenworth / WVM&CC / Brender Collection #003-60-74*

FAR BELOW: The Peavine was a logging railroad which went up the Chumstick Canyon, over Beaver Hill and into Plain. It was built to access Lamb-Davis forest land. *Courtesy Byron Dickinson Collection*

RIGHT: Stevens Pass Highway through Tumwater Canyon. Photo, circa 1930. *Courtesy Bill Haines Collection*

ABOVE LEFT: James C. Buchanan, telegraph lineman with the Great Northern Railway for 45 years. *Courtesy Eugene Buchanan Collection*

BELOW LEFT: The first train through the Wellington disaster site. *Courtesy Byron Dickinson Collection*

ABOVE: This trestle remained after the Peavine Railroad was discontinued. This view is from Beaver hill looking into Plain. *Courtesy Byron Dickinson Collection*

BELOW: The Pobst dairy in Plain was a successful venture for many years. Pictured is O.M. Pobst. *Courtesy Byron Dickinson Collection*

OPPOSITE: A.C. Barclay and family, owners of the Barclay Hotel. The first car through Tumwater Canyon to Chiwaukum on the old G.N. grade, August 9, 1929. *Courtesy Marv Speer Collection*

Recreation

From earliest times town baseball teams were a feature of most small towns and Leavenworth was no exception. Those playing were clerks, newsmen, dray operators, etc., all fully grown men. Often a town band accompanied them on their travels. A crowd of supporters attended every game.

Football came when state law ruled all youngsters must have physical education. Gymnasiums sprouted in every town and while they were being put up, football teams worked out. Most of the students played, for it was largely a college sport before 1920.

With the gymnasium, which was also built as a community building, boys and girls learned basketball. Baseball was overshadowed by competitions by school teams in their sports. Leavenworth basketball teams were superior, attracting a crowd of sports-loving fans during the Twenties.

Few in town knew anything of skiing unless they had a northern European heritage. Fortunately a number did. The first ski jump was a display of the art. It soon matured into a huge annual event with trains bringing in spectators and competition adding considerable spice to the program. This was our first real taste of tourism, and it was wholeheartedly supported.

LEFT: Henry Harrison and Leonard Frost log rolling at the fair on the Fourth of July, 1926, at the G.N. mill pond. *Courtesy Stan Harrison Collection*

Later, teaching skiing to youngsters made the winter sport well known. Cross-country skiing over local trails has put even more on skis.

One of the most memorable events in the region was the movie filmed while the sawmill was in operation and based on James Oliver Curwood's book, "The Ancient Highway". Some was filmed in the valley, more at Lake Wenatchee and the Chiwawa River. Local folks played extras and found the close contact with movie stars refreshing and enlightening.

From early times celebrating the Fourth of July was a big thing. Towns took turns at staging the several day event with races, band performances, baseball, speeches, picnicking, etc. Workers were given time off from their jobs and the town was full of those who came to celebrate.

An annual picnic held by the old settlers was an annual affair enjoyed by many for a time. The first was held in a school, the next several in wooded spots reached by the logging railroad.

Not so large, but a favorite, were the church Christmas celebrations that eventually led to a town Christmas tree in the park before families each had their own gaily decorated tree and individual gift giving. For many years the Christmas Lighting ceremony, when all the town turned on its holiday lights at the same time, drew capacity crowds.

Sportsmen enjoy fishing, rock climbing, hiking nearby, while the town pool attracts a capacity crowd of "younguns" during the hot summer days.

ABOVE: Peshastin baseball team, circa 1939. *Courtesy Helen Hauff Link Collection*

NEAR RIGHT: Icicle River camping trip. *Courtesy Fran Wise Collection*

FAR RIGHT: Alta Williams at a ball game in Leavenworth (she is fifth from right). *Courtesy Fran Wise Collection*

LEFT: Camping trip near Leavenworth, circa 1910. *Courtesy Fran Wise Collection*
BELOW: A group of women enjoying a beautiful day near Leavenworth. *Courtesy Fran Wise Collection*

ABOVE: A fight scene in the silent movie production "The Ancient Highway." Locals figured prominently in the film as extras. *Courtesy Byron Dickinson Collection*

BELOW: Billy Dove, famous silent screen actress, in Leavenworth. *Courtesy Byron Dickinson Collection*

RIGHT: Silent screen stars Billy Dove and Jack Holt in Leavenworth for the filming of "The Ancient Highway." *Courtesy Byron Dickinson Collection*

BELOW RIGHT: Billy Dove and Jack Holt filming a rescue scene in the Chiwawa River for the silent screen movie "The Ancient Highway." *Courtesy Byron Dickinson Collection*

LEFT: Mrs. Gutherless with a fish she caught at Peshastin Creek, circa 1915. *Courtesy Bill Haines Collection*

ABOVE: Exploring Tumwater Canyon, circa 1915. *Courtesy Fran Wise Collection*

OPPOSITE: Wenatchee River near Leavenworth, 1916. *Courtesy Fran Wise Collection*

OPPOSITE: Leavenworth All Star Team of 1921, Champions of the Northwest. This Leavenworth team beat the Seattle team who claimed to be the champions of the Pacific Northwest. Standing is Ross Mcnett, Ed Hoxey, Al Hoffman, Doc Osborn, and Joe Smith. In the front is Tuffey Wunder, Bruce Smith, Bill Wunder, Swede Nelson. Ed Hoxey was Dr. George Hoxey's brother. Doc Osborn became Superintendent of Schools in Leavenworth. The town honored him by naming the John H. Osborn Elementary School for him. *Courtesy John B. Smith Collection*
ABOVE: Leavenworth All Star basketball team, 1924. *Courtesy Upper Valley Museum at Leavenworth Collection*
RIGHT: Ben, Ted and Dave Parsons, 1940s. *Upper Valley Museum at Leavenworth / WVM&CC / Parsons Collection*
#003-77-7

ABOVE: Alta and Floyd Williams with a friend, circa 1923. *Courtesy Fran Wise Collection*
RIGHT: The old ski hill parking lot, circa 1929. *Courtesy Stan Harrison Collection*

FAR ABOVE: Ingalls Creek Lodge and service station; woman on skis identified as "Agnes," 1938. *Upper Valley Museum at Leavenworth / WVM&CC / Brender Collection #003-60-94*

ABOVE RIGHT: "Ski Special" train in Leavenworth for ski jump event; 1938. *Upper Valley Museum at Leavenworth / WVM&CC / Brender Collection #003-60-77*

NEAR ABOVE: Unidentified women sledders at Leavenworth. *Upper Valley Museum at Leavenworth / WVM&CC / Brender Collection #003-60-31*

RIGHT: Crowds of people at Leavenworth Ski Hill, 1938. *Upper Valley Museum at Leavenworth / WVM&CC / Brender Collection #003-60-79*

OPPOSITE: Boy Scout Troup #2 in Leavenworth. Scout in the center holding the trophy is Roy Hatmaker, circa 1922.

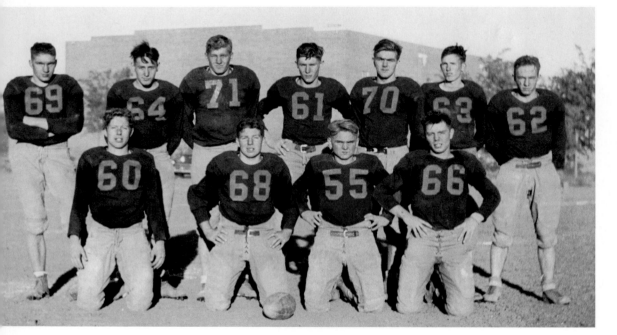

ABOVE LEFT: Wilson Walton, Leavenworth High School football, 1925-1926; oldest son of Bill and Rose Walton. *Wenatchee Valley Museum & Cultural Center / Walton Collection #81-115-4*

ABOVE MIDDLE: Ski Hill "A" jump, 1950s. *Upper Valley Museum at Leavenworth / WVM&CC / Parsons Collection #003-77-15*

ABOVE RIGHT: Chickamin Tribe #97, Leavenworth, Washington. John H. Stevens, third from left; note a bell tower, Leavenworth Echo building, and The Tumwater Hotel visible in background. *Wenatchee Valley Museum & Cultural Center / Stevens Collection #78-208-31*

LEFT: 1948 Leavenworth football team posed kneeling and standing identified from left, kneeling: Bob Ferguson, Vern Rae, Arnie Sweat, and Bill Ferguson; standing: Pet Hanson, Kenny Buzzard, Willard West, Dave Parsons, Del Sagaser, Bill Hollingsworth and Rod Franklin. Photo taken at Ephrata after the game where Leavenworth won 24-0. *Upper Valley Museum at Leavenworth / WVM&CC / Parsley Collection #004-26-3*

OPPOSITE: Swimming party at Lake Wenatchee, August 18, 1901. *Wenatchee Valley Museum & Cultural Center / Adams Collection #84-30-5*

ABOVE LEFT: In the 1920s and 1930s, a few men supplemented their meager means by trapping. These two spent the winter trapping pine marten in the Upper Chiwawa. *Courtesy Byron Dickinson Collection*

ABOVE: River drivers in the early 1920s. The boats were called bateaus and carried the men along the Wenatchee and Chiwawa River. *Courtesy Byron Dickinson Collection*

LEFT: Leavenworth's float, "Flowers of the Foothills" won the Grand Sweepstakes in the 1927 Apple Blossom Festival Parade. Riding were Princess Helen Field and her attendants Margaret Rutherford and Anna Day. Frank Motteler drove the float. *Courtesy Chamber of Commerce Collection*

RIGHT: Skier jumping at the old ski hill, 1926. *Courtesy Stan Harrison Collection*

OPPOSITE: The old ski hill, circa 1929. *Courtesy Stan Harrison Collection*

ABOVE: Gutherless family picnic at Cougar Inn, 1927. *Courtesy Bill Haines Collection*

FAR LEFT: The first ski jump tournament held in Leavenworth, February 10, 1929. Segard Hanson was the winner of Class A with a jump of 65 feet. *Courtesy Margaret "Mom" Miller Collection*

NEAR LEFT: John Hauff Sr. and the 1939 Hauff family basketball team. The sons are, left to right, Albert, Irving, John, Fred, Emil, and Bill. *Courtesy Helen Hauff Link Collection*

ABOVE: Leavenworth Last Supper, January 1, 1916. Left to right, back row, Bill Atwood, M. Marley, Art Johnson, Max Kringle, Daddy Day, F. Williams, (bartender) Hogan, Mr. Hadley, C. Campbell, F. Wingate, John McKinnon. Front row, Jack Farrell, B. Rutherford, Ed Tholin, Sam Potter, M. Moore, C. Norberg, Dr. Hoxsey, Bill Watson, Jack Carr, Dr. Judah.

ABOVE: Early Leavenworth not only had a baseball team, but a stadium as well. Rattlesnake Mountain is in the background. *Courtesy Byron Dickinson Collection*

LEFT: Bill, Carol and Barbara Burgess show off a salmon they caught in the Wenatchee River. *Courtesy Byron Dickinson Collection*

RIGHT: Baseball Boys Dinner given by Mrs. G.W. (Ida) Hoxsey and Mrs. J.D. Elliott, Leavenworth, 1910. Left side of table, front to back: John "Jack" Mahoney - centerfield; Jimmie Coulsen - sub; Dr. George W. Hoxsey; L. Hontous - 1st base; Jimmie Miller - shortstop; J. Edward "Eddie" Tholin - 2nd base; Charlie Keppler - 3rd base; either Ned Raymond or Joe Peltier - leftfield; Mr. Smoker. Right side of table, front to back: Jerome Sonders - catcher; Bobbie Smith - right field; Tom Burke; Fred Lee - pitcher; J.W. Elliot; Jack Carr; Mr. McDonald; Harry Krollpfeiffer; Mr. Carlquist.
Wenatchee Valley Museum & Cultural Center / Adams Collection #84-30-17

LEFT: Ralph Newell trying to hold down his end of the bench. *Courtesy Byron Dickinson Collection*

NEAR BELOW: Leavenworth Winter Sports Club float won the Apple Blossom Festival Grand Sweepstakes, 1931. Riding on the float are Yvonne Penderast, Bobbie Hearst, Peggy Taylor, Joy Smith, Jean Field, Mary McDermott, Jane Gillis and Lila Mae Jones. *Courtesy Chamber of Commerce Collection*

FAR BELOW: Leavenworth ski jump, 1931. *Courtesy Chamber of Commerce Collection*

ABOVE: The Alps Tourist Park in Tumwater Canyon, circa 1932, owned by W. E. Hansen. *Courtesy Blackburn Family Collection*

LEFT: Near The Alps Tourist Park in Tumwater Canyon, circa 1932. *Courtesy Blackburn Family Collection*

RIGHT: The Alps in Tumwater Canyon, circa 1932. Hazel Hansen and her mother on the lake behind the Tumwater Dam. Hazel was a former Chamber of Commerce secretary. *Courtesy Blackburn Family Collection*

FAR ABOVE: People from Seattle who arrived by train are loaded onto trucks, cars and buses downtown. They were on their way to the ski hill for the 1932 Ski Tournament. *Courtesy Margaret "Mom" Miller Collection*

NEAR ABOVE: Camp at the head of Icicle Creek for crew constructing the Cascade Crest Trail, 1934. *Courtesy Kjell Bakke Collection*

RIGHT: The skiing sweathearts, 1932. Carolyn Krillfeiffer, Lila Mae Jones, Mary McDermott, and Joy Smith. *Courtesy Margaret "Mom" Miller Collection*

LEFT: Merritt, 1936. Left to right: Ethel (Bakke) Gehring, Kjell Bakke, Marie (Bakke) Bremner. *Courtesy Kjell Bakke Collection*
ABOVE: Kjell Bakke at age three at the Leavenworth Ski Hill, 1936. *Courtesy Kjell Bakke Collection*

LEFT: Dr. and Mrs. Marvin Speer Jr. at Fish Lake 1937. Their first spring in Leavenworth. *Courtesy Speer Family Collection*
BELOW LEFT: Dr. and Mrs. Speer Jr. at White Pine near Rayrock, 1937. *Courtesy Speer Family Collection*
BELOW: Doctor Hopkins with his horse on the ranch between Ski Hill Drive and Titus Road. *Courtesy Rena Stroup Collection*

ABOVE LEFT: Peshastin Lumber and Box Mill annual union and family picnic circa 1940. *Courtesy Helen Hauff Link Collection*

LEFT: Fish Lake, circa 1940. Left to right: Wilson, John and Jim Evans. *Courtesy Carol Thorson Collection*

ABOVE RIGHT: Marten pelts held by Dudley Wilson. *Courtesy Judy Wyssen Collection*

OPPOSITE: Apple Box Tournament, 1939. 200 Leavenworth citizens handed apple boxes full of snow to each other up the hill for about two days and then sent the empty boxes back down in the chute on the other side of the landing hill. Due to lack of snow, the tournament would have been cancelled had the citizens not rallied by hauling snow from the mountains. *Courtesy Margaret "Mom" Miller Collection*

ABOVE: 1940 Ski Tournament. *Courtesy Margaret "Mom" Miller Collection*
ABOVE RIGHT: W.O. Burgess caught this fox in a trap and made a pet of it, until the price of fur went up. *Courtesy Byron Dickinson Collection*
BELOW RIGHT: Torger Tokle, 1941, North American Ski Tournament, record, 273 feet. *Courtesy Margaret "Mom" Miller Collection*

ABOVE: Lake Wenatchee Ranger Ray Kellicut (second from right) helps the W.O. Burgess clan with their watermelon crop. *Courtesy Byron Dickinson Collection*

NEAR RIGHT: Dudley Wilson when trapping up Chiwaukum and Entiat Ridge for marten, 1945. *Courtesy Sylvia Lance Collection*

FAR RIGHT: Trapping cabin in summer at French Creek up the Icicle. Otis Buzard, 1944. *Courtesy Leah Wilson-Smith Collection*

ABOVE: Peshastin Lumberjacks basketball team, 1947. *Courtesy Helen Hauff Link Collection*
LEFT: Paul Gasprich, Joe Koselisky and Bill Maa find an appropriate boxing ring to express some youthful prowess. Members of the Camp Icicle, Company 983rd, Civilian Conservation Corps, circa 1935. *Courtesy Upper Valley Museum at Leavenworth / WVM&CC / C.C.C Collection #003-82-131*
OPPOSITE: Leavenworth High School ski team, 1949. All these skiers competed in jumping, cross country, downhill, and slalom. They were champions in jumping, cross country, and four way combined. Left to right, Lincoln McPherson (school faculty representative), Max Scofield, Jim Vincent, Kjell Bakke, Ken Wood, Jack Haugh, Earl Johnson, Paul Hatmaker (coach). *Courtesy Kjell Bakke Collection*

LEFT: Leavenworth B and C Jump, circa 1950. *Courtesy Kjell Bakke Collection*
ABOVE & BELOW: Leavenworth Rodeo. The county fairgrounds, race track and rodeos were held at the site which today is the golf course. Later, rodeos were held at the end of Poplar Street.